ROTHERHAM LIBRARY & INFORMATION SERVICES

This book must be returned by the date specified at the time of issue as the DATE DUE FOR RETURN.

The loan may be extended (personally, by post or telephone) for a further period if the book is not required by another reader, by quoting the above number / author / title.

LIS7a

D1639752

Titles in this series
Don't Call Me Special – a first look at disability
I Miss You – a first look at death
My Amazing Body – a first look at health and fitness
My Amazing Journey – a first look at where babies come from
My Brother, My Sister and Me – a first look at sibling rivalry
My Family's Changing – a first look at family break-up
My Friends and Me – a first look at friendship
Stop Picking on Me – a first look at bullying

Text copyright © Pat Thomas 2001
Illustrations copyright © Lesley Harker 2001

Series concept: Lisa Edwards
Editor: Liz Gogerly
Concept design: Kate Buxton
Design: Jean Wheeler

Published in Great Britain by Hodder Wayland,
an imprint of Hodder Children's Books

British Library Cataloguing in Publication Data

Thomas, Pat, 1959-
First look at diet and health
1.Health
I.Title II.Harker, Lesley III.Diet and health
613

ISBN 0 7502 3557 8

Printed in Hong Kong by Wing King Tong

Hodder Children's Books
A division of Hodder Headline Limited
338 Euston Road
London NW1 3BH

My Amazing Body

A FIRST LOOK AT HEALTH AND FITNESS

PAT THOMAS
ILLUSTRATED BY LESLEY HARKER

HODDER
Wayland

You have an amazing body.

So do all the other people
in the world.

You have a brain which can do more complicated thinking than any computer.

You have a body which can
move in more different ways
than any robot.

You have five senses – sight,
hearing, taste, touch and smell –
that tell you lots of important things
about the world around you
without you even having to ask.

Your body can do lots of other things on its own too.
Your heart beats, your lungs breathe –

and when you graze your knee or get a cold, your body
can make you well again without you having to tell it to.

But your body can't do
everything on its own.
It needs some help
from you.

There are lots of ways you can help your body stay fit and healthy. All of them are easy and most of them are fun as well.

What about you?

How many different things can you think of that help keep your body healthy? How often do you do these things?

Food contains vitamins, minerals and energy. These things help you to think and play and grow.

When you eat fresh fruits and vegetables
and protein foods like meat, milk
and beans you are giving your
body the things it
needs to grow.

But when you eat lots of sweets, crisps and fizzy drinks you are not giving your body the nutrients it needs.

These foods and drinks may taste nice but if you have them too often your body may become sick.

It's OK to eat these foods sometimes. But the best way to stay healthy is to eat lots of different kinds of foods every day.

Another way to help your body is to use it in every way you can. That means getting lots of exercise. Exercise helps your muscles to stay strong and fit, and helps your bones to grow.

18

When you are running and jumping and stretching you are exercising your heart and helping it to pump blood all over your body. You are also exercising your lungs, helping them to breathe in more air.

What about you?

Do you like to run and jump around?
What are your favourite types of exercise?
How often do you get to do these things?

There are other good ways
to help your body
stay healthy.

When you bathe and brush your teeth you are
helping keep yourself clean and free from germs.

And while exercising
is good, resting is
important too.

We all need plenty of sleep and to have times
when we can work or play quietly.

21

Your body is always giving you clues about what it needs.

When your body needs rest, you feel tired.

When your body needs food, you feel hungry.

And when your body has had enough food, you feel full.

When you feel a pain it's a message that a part of you needs care and attention. It's important to listen to the messages your body is sending you.

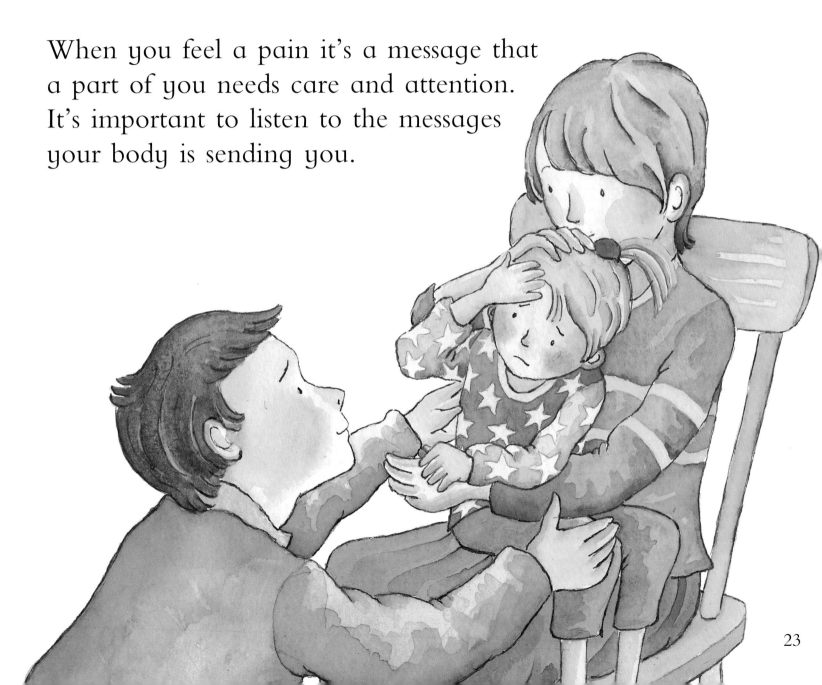

Even healthy people get ill sometimes. It's never nice to get sick, but when you are sick your body is doing something amazing.

It is making a memory of that illness, so that next time
you can get better more quickly.

You only have one body and it is the most important thing you will ever own.

26

Your body is built
to last you a long time. And if
you take really good care of it, it will.

FURTHER INFORMATION

Children often imitate adults when it comes to eating habits. If parents are rarely seen eating fresh fruits and vegetables or freshly prepared meals, children will learn that this is the correct way to eat. Pre-packaged foods are convenient but are often nutritionally poor. As often as is practical parents should strive to put fresh food on the table. Likewise, children usually copy their parents' exercise habits. To encourage your child to get up and move, you may have to do the same. Special activities for children such as the Saturday gym or swimming are great. But regular activities that all the family can enjoy are also a good way of encouraging your child to be active.

There is an argument that, for small children, several small meals throughout the day is a better way to maintain health and absorb nutrients since it places less stress on the digestive system. While there is a place in most diets for crisps and chocolates, these need to be balanced by healthier alternatives. A well-chosen snack can also ward off the extreme hunger which can lead to continual cravings and bingeing on the wrong kinds of foods. Often children will eat whatever is around, so it's best to make sure there is always a bowl of colourful fruit on hand for children to choose from.

Food fads and a decreased appetite are normal during childhood. As your child's growth slows down, appetite will also decline. While it may seem that your child is not eating enough, it is highly unlikely that your child's appetite will decrease to such an extent that their health is compromised. At some point during the pre-school years many children go through another growth spurt. Take advantage of your child's increased appetite at this time and introduce a greater variety of healthier food options based on freshly prepared dishes and unprocessed wholefoods.

Schools are well placed to teach about diet and fitness from many different angles. Exploring different religious customs which involve food, or finding out about the foods people from other cultures eat can broaden children's horizons considerably. Similarly, introducing a wide range of PE or playground activities can aid children in finding a sport which suits them. Some schools have found that introducing a 'fruit time' in the afternoon is influential. Once children leave nursery they often don't have an afternoon break of this nature. A ten-minute break in the afternoon for the class to snack on fruit or vegetables can improve energy levels and help to reinforce good eating habits.

GLOSSARY

Nutrients The vitamins and minerals in your food are known as nutrients. These are the things your body needs to grow and stay healthy.

Energy Energy is the fuel that makes your body work properly. Your food provides the energy that powers your brain, your muscles and all the other parts of your body.

Germs Germs are living things which are too small to see. They don't usually cause problems unless your body is weakened by eating the wrong foods or not getting enough sleep. When this happens, germs can cause illnesses like colds and tummy upsets.

BOOKS TO READ

Non-fiction
Am I Fit and Healthy? by Claire Llewelyn and Mike Gordon (Hodder Wayland, 1998)

Breakfast, Lunch and Evening Meals by Gill Munton – three titles which are part of the *Food Around the World* series. (Hodder Wayland, 1998)

Exercise and Health by Jillian Powell – titles available in the *Health Matters* series (Hodder Wayland, 1997)

I'm Happy, I'm Healthy! by Alex Parsons – titles from the *Life Education* series (Franklin Watts, 1996)

Fiction
Oliver's Fruit Salad by Vivian French and Alison Barlett (Hodder Wayland, 1999)

Eek! Fly Trap by Anastasio/Cooper (Heinemann, 2000)

The Very Hungry Caterpillar by Eric Carle (Puffin, 1995)

USEFUL CONTACTS

British Nutrition Foundation
High Holborn House
52-54 High Holborn
London WC1V 6RQ
Tel: 0207 404 6504
Provides information and advice about nutrition for people of all ages.

The Vegetarian Society
Parkdale
Dunham Road
Altrincham
Cheshire WA14 4QG
Tel: 0161 928 0793
Offers advice and information sheets about being a vegetarian.